STAGE 2

Let's Go Rock Collecting

by Roma Gans • illustrated by Holly Keller

HarperCollinsPublishers

With special thanks to Laurence Lippsett and Linda Sohl for their expert advice.

The illustrations in this book were created with pen and ink, watercolors, and pastels on Rives BFK paper.

The *Let's-Read-and-Find-Out Science* book series was originated by Dr. Franklyn M. Branley, Astronomer Emeritus and former Chairman of the American Museum–Hayden Planetarium, and was formerly co-edited by him and Dr. Roma Gans, Professor Emeritus of Childhood Education, Teachers College, Columbia University. Text and illustrations for each of the books in the series are checked for accuracy by an expert in the relevant field. For more information about Let's-Read-and-Find-Out Science books, write to HarperCollins Children's Books, 10 East 53rd Street, New York, NY 10022.

Library of Congress Cataloging-in-Publication Data
Gans, Roma, date
    Let's go rock collecting / by Roma Gans ; illustrated by Holly Keller. — [2nd ed.]
      p.   cm. — (Let's-read-and-find-out science. Stage 1)
    Summary: Describes the formation and characteristics of igneous, metamorphic, and sedimentary rocks and how to recognize and collect them.
    ISBN 0-06-027282-1. — ISBN 0-06-027283-X (lib. bdg.) — ISBN 0-06-445170-4 (pbk.)
    1. Rocks—Collection and preservation—Juvenile literature.   [1. Rocks—Collection and preservation.]
I. Keller, Holly, ill.   II. Title.   III. Series.
QE433.6.G36   1997   95-44999
552'.0075—dc20   CIP
                                                                                 AC

Let's Go Rock Collecting

People collect all kinds of things. They collect coins, stamps, baseball cards, shells, toys, bottles, pictures, and cats. Some people collect things that are very old—the older the better.

The oldest things you can collect are rocks. Most of them are millions and millions of years old. Most kinds of rocks are easy to find. But some, like diamonds and emeralds, are rare. That's why they are valuable.

CRUST

SOLID ROCK LAYER

8

Rocks cover the whole earth. No matter where you live, you live on rock.

There is rock under city streets and country farms. And there is rock under every ocean, lake, and river.

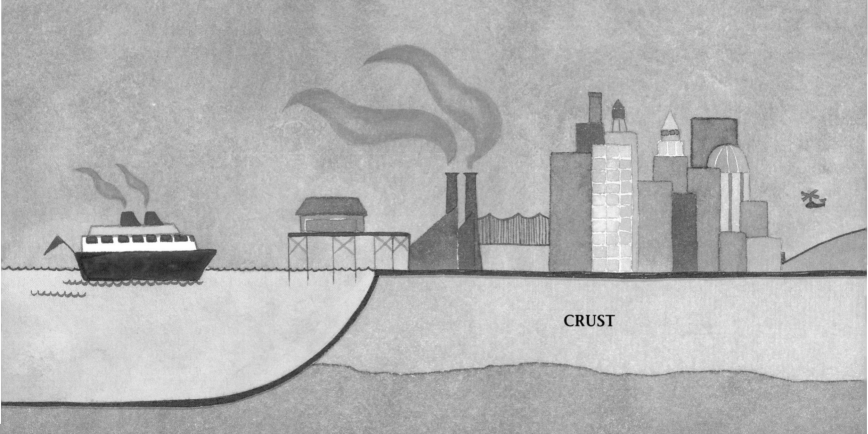

CRUST

The Romans built roads out of rocks. The roads are still used today. Things made with rocks last and last.

The rocks that make up the surface of the earth are called the earth's crust. Most of the crust is made of igneous rock. Igneous means made by heat.

Inside the earth it is very hot—hot enough to melt rock. The melted rock is called magma.

Sometimes the magma pushes through cracks in the crust. When magma comes to the surface, it is called lava. The lava cools and becomes very hard. It becomes igneous rock. Most of the earth's igneous rock comes from volcanoes on the seafloor.

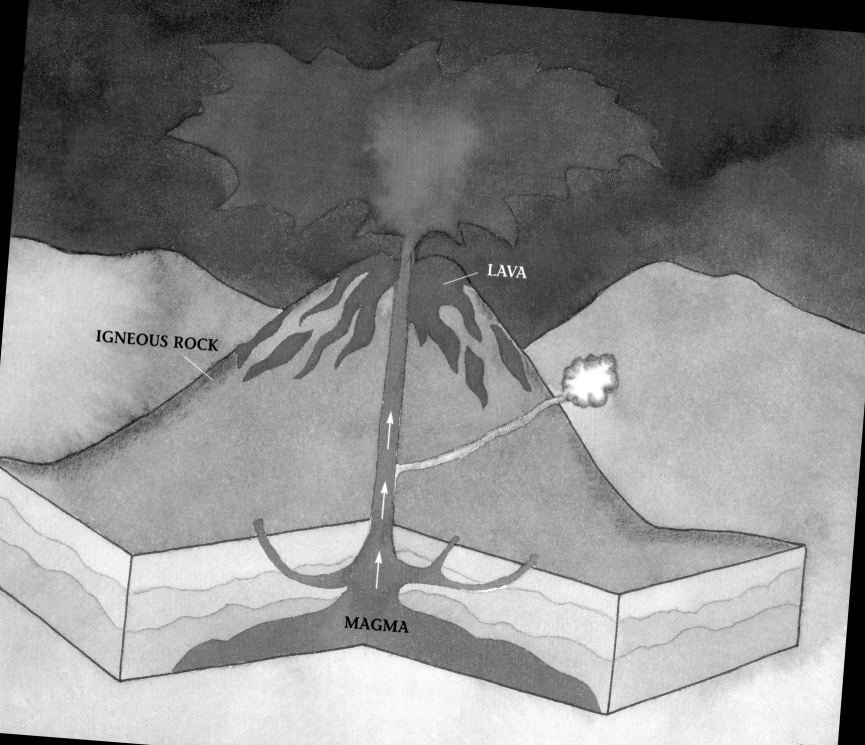

LAVA

IGNEOUS ROCK

MAGMA

GRANITE

Granite is an igneous rock. It once was magma. Some granite is gray with small, shiny black and white crystals. Some granite has large pink, black, and white crystals.

QUARTZ

The crystals in granite are called quartz. Some pieces of quartz are white like milk. Others are clear like glass.

14

QUARTZ

Sometimes quartz has bands of many colors. Jewelry is made from it. The marbles you play with may be made of banded quartz.

BASALT

Basalt is another kind of igneous rock. It is usually dark in color— gray, green, or black. It is the most common of all igneous rocks.

MOHS' SCALE OF HARDNESS

SOFT

| 1. TALC | 2. GYPSUM | 3. CALCITE | 4. FLUORITE | 5. APATITE |

Not all rocks are hard. Some rocks are soft. Talc is
so soft, you can pinch it into powder with your fingers.
Talc is number 1 on a scale for hardness of rocks.
The scale is called "Mohs' scale of hardness," and it
goes from 1 to 10. Quartz is number 7. Diamonds are

HARD

6. ORTHOCLASE 7. QUARTZ 8. TOPAZ 9. CORUNDUM 10. DIAMOND

number 10. They are the hardest rocks in the world.
Each mineral on the scale can scratch the mineral
below it. A fingernail has a hardness of about $2\frac{1}{2}$.
So your fingernail can leave a scratch in talc, but
not in calcite.

SAND, MUD, PEBBLES

SAND, MUD, PEBBLES

SAND, MUD, PEBBLES

SEDIMENTARY ROCK FORMING

Not all rocks are igneous rocks. Some are made of sediments. Sandstone is one kind of sedimentary rock. It is made of grains of sand, mud, and pebbles.

Millions of years ago, sand was blown into rivers. The rivers carried the sand along and dropped it into lakes or oceans. Layer after layer settled on the bottoms of the lakes and seas. The top layers pressed down on the bottom layers. Slowly the lower layers of sand became stone.

You'll know sandstone when you see it. It is often soft and grainy. Rub it with your fingers, and grains of sand may come off.

Another sedimentary rock is limestone. It is made of the shells of animals that lived millions of years ago. Most often, limestone is white. But it can be pink, tan, and other colors. Sometimes you can see the outlines of shells in limestone.

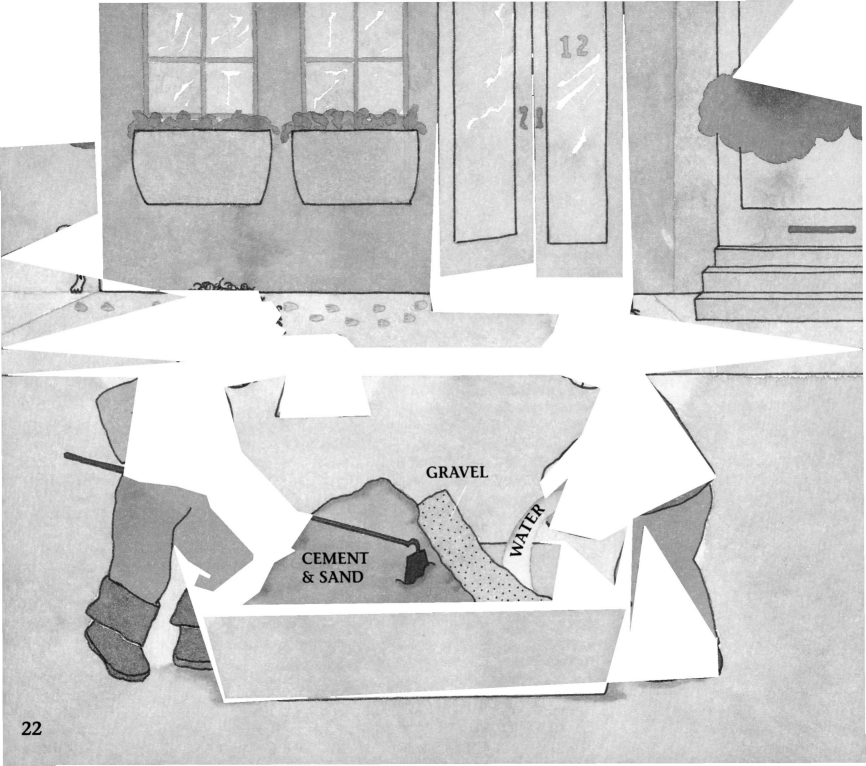

GRAVEL

CEMENT
& SAND

WATER

Limestone is used to make cement. Cement
is then mixed with sand, gravel, and water to make
concrete for sidewalks.

Five thousand years ago the Egyptians built the
pyramids out of limestone. They are still standing.
Maybe someday you'll go to Egypt and see them.

Besides igneous and sedimentary rocks, there is a third kind of rock in the earth's crust. It is called metamorphic. Metamorphic means changed.

Slate is a metamorphic rock. Slate was once shale.

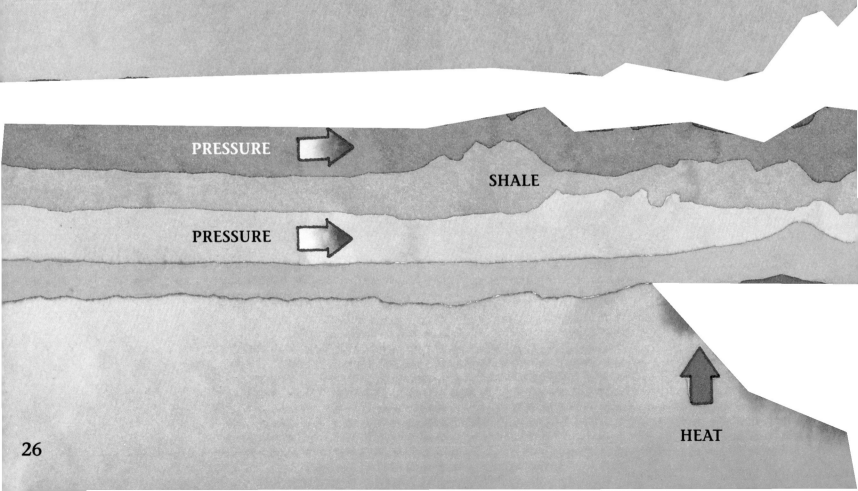

PRESSURE

SHALE

PRESSURE

HEAT

But over millions of years, tons and tons of rock pressed on it. The pressure made the shale very hot, and the heat and pressure changed it into slate. Most slate is gray, but some is black, red, or brown.

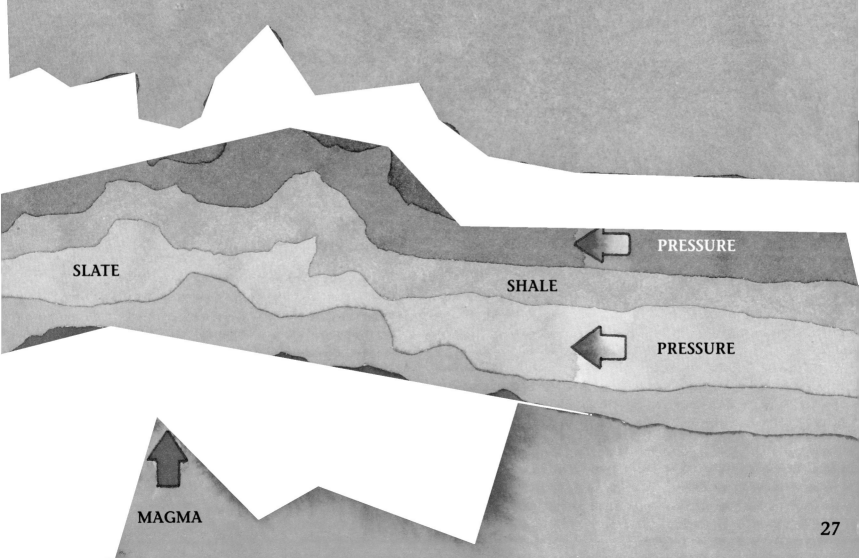

SLATE

PRESSURE

SHALE

PRESSURE

MAGMA

Other metamorphic rocks are made the same way slate is, by heat and pressure. Some metamorphic rocks are so changed, you can't tell what they once were.

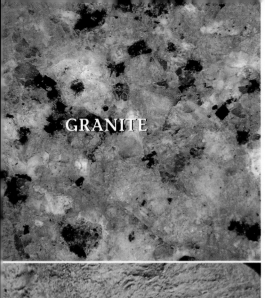

GRANITE

Granite can turn into gneiss. It once was a piece of gray granite. Now it is darker gray, and its crystals have separated into layers.

GNEISS

LIMESTONE

Limestone turns into marble. Some marble has colored marks that look like clouds.

MARBLE

SANDSTONE

Sandstone turns into quartzite. It may still look like sedimentary sandstone, but now it is much harder.

QUARTZITE

When you start collecting rocks, you'll find out how many different varieties there are. One way to start a collection is to look for rocks of different colors. You'll find there are pink rocks, black rocks, and pure white ones. There are gray rocks, and brown and yellow ones. See if you can tell what kind of rocks they are.

You can keep your small rocks in egg cartons.

You can keep larger ones in cardboard boxes with dividers like this one.

Rock collecting is fun. And one of the best things about it is that you can do it anywhere. Wherever you go, try to find new rocks and add them to your collection.